# Green Planet

**LEVEL TWO**  **700 HEADWORDS**

# OXFORD

UNIVERSITY PRESS

Great Clarendon Street, Oxford OX2 6DP

Oxford University Press is a department of the University of Oxford. It furthers the University's objective of excellence in research, scholarship, and education by publishing worldwide in

Oxford  New York

Auckland  Cape Town  Dar es Salaam  Hong Kong  Karachi
Kuala Lumpur  Madrid  Melbourne  Mexico City  Nairobi
New Delhi  Shanghai  Taipei  Toronto

With offices in

Argentina  Austria  Brazil  Chile  Czech Republic  France
Greece  Guatemala  Hungary  Italy  Japan  Poland  Portugal
Singapore  South Korea  Switzerland  Thailand  Turkey
Ukraine  Vietnam

OXFORD and OXFORD ENGLISH are registered trade marks of Oxford University Press in the UK and in certain other countries

© Oxford University Press 2010

The moral rights of the author have been asserted

Database right Oxford University Press (maker)

First published in Dominoes 2004

2015

20 19 18 17 16 15

ISBN: 978 0 19 424891 4  Book
ISBN: 978 0 19 424843 3  Book and MultiROM Pack
MultiROM not available separately

ACKNOWLEDGEMENTS

The publisher would like to thank the following for permission to reproduce photographs: Alamy Images pp15 (Humpback whale/Stephen Frink Collection), 20 (Lemons/Andre Jenny), 20 (Chocolate/Maximilian Stock/Anthony Blake Photo Library), 20 (Coconut/Nicholas Pitt/Travelsnaps), 20 (Sugar cane/J Marshall - Tribaleye Images), 36 (A Can of Tuna Fish/Foodcollection.com), 51 (Child drinking water/Robert Harding Picture Library); Aquarius Library p35 (Finding Nemo/Walt Disney); Corbis ppiv (Trilobite fossil/Layne Kennedy), iv (Collapsed freeway/Jim Sugar), 7 (Rachel Carson/Bettmann), 7 (Leonardo DiCaprio/ Reuters), 7 (Julian Huxley/Hulton-Deutsch Collection), 10 (Panda/Keren Su), 20 (Cocoa pods/Bob Krist), 20 (Vanilla bean pods/Owen Franken), 25 (Bison/Layne Kennedy), 25 (Yellowstone National Park entrance/L.Clarke), 26 (Bison/ Layne Kennedy), 28 (John Muir/Bettmann), 31 (Emperor Penguin/Galen Rowell), 33 (adeli penguins/Zefa), 42 (Workers cleaning oil-covered rocks/Natalie Fobes), 57 (Mount Everest), 63 (adeli penguins/Zefa); Dover Books p6 (finch); Evolution Film/Denise Zemikhol pp23 (rubber tapping), 23 (Chico Mendes); Getty Images pp19 (Sopo'aga Falls and rainforest/Tom Hill/Stone), 27 (Fish swimming over coral reef/Jeff Hunter/Photographer's Choice), 29 (Jaguar/Art Wolfe), 35 (Polar bear/Darrell Gulin), 40 (Orca Whale/Brandon Cole), 48 (Beijing traffic/Kim Steele), 50 (Wind farm/Pat LaCroix), 52 (Malnourished child/Ami Vitale), 62 (Sopo'aga Falls and rainforest/Tom Hill/Stone); Greenpeace UK Picture Desk pp14 (Phyllis Cormack,1971), 16 (Rainbow Warrior sunk in Auckland Harbour), 61 (Rainbow Warrior sunk in Auckland Harbour); Interface Europe Ltd. p55 (Corn cob carpet tiles); iStockphoto p47 (City bikers/Can Balcioglu); Mary Evans Picture Library p3 (Darwin/Finch/Galapagos); NASA pp iv (Saturn with rings), iv (Earth), 1 (Rocket launching Envisat), 1 (Envisat satellite), 7 (Earth), 64 (Envisat satellite); National Oceanic and Atmospheric Administration Photo Library pp36 (helicopter), 36 (Tuna fishing); Natural History Photography p20 (Brazil nut on tree/ Andre Baetschi); NHPA p20 (Cola nut); OUP pp iv(Coral reef/Corel), iv(Houses in floodwater/JupiterImages/ Comstock), iv (Forest/Photodisc), iv (Ice/Photodisc), 20 (Coconut/Photodisc), 20 (Cola drink), 20 (Brazil nuts/ Stockbyte), 20 (Sugar in bowl), 24 (Leaves/Digital Vision), 30 (Grand Canyon/Corel), 31 (Polar bear/Digital Vision), 40 (Bald Eagle/Photodisc), 40 (Sea otter/Corel), 56 (Great Barrier Reef/Corbis/Digital Stock), 67 (Polar bear/Digital Vision); Photolibrary pp12 (Caribbean beach/Kerrigan Scott), 20 (Vanilla beans/Photononstop), 21 (Golden toad/ Michael Modgen), 25 (Jaguar/David Cayless), 31 (Dolphins/ Mike Hill); Press Association Images pp9 (Parachutes), 39 (Chernobyl reactor), 44 (Chernobyl after explosion), 58 (Oil barrier), 59 (Beach clean-up), 59 (Oiled bird), 59 (Prestige tanker broken in two), 59 (Beach covered in oil), 65 (Beach covered in oil), 66 (Chernobyl after explosion); Reuters Pictures p53 (School children given free vitamins/ Romeo Ranoco); Rex Features pp18 (Explosion), 41 (Exxon Waldex/Sipa Press), 58 (Submarine 'Nautile'/Sipa Press); Steve Winter p29 (Alan Rabinovitz); TreePeople p55 (tree-planting/Thom Anable); WWF p10 (logo).

Cover: Getty Images (Rainforest vegetation/R H Productions)

Illustrations by: Paul Gardiner pp4, 9.

**DOMINOES**

Series Editors: Bill Bowler and Sue Parminter

# Green Planet

*Christine Lindop*

Christine Lindop was born in New Zealand, and taught English in France and Spain before settling in Great Britain. She has written and adapted more than twenty books, including *Australia and New Zealand* in the Oxford Bookworms series, and *The Turn of the Screw* in the Dominoes series. In her free time she likes reading, watching films, and making mosaics. Her favourite part of this planet is her vegetable and fruit garden, which is 'as big as a swimming pool, and just as much fun'.

**OXFORD**
UNIVERSITY PRESS

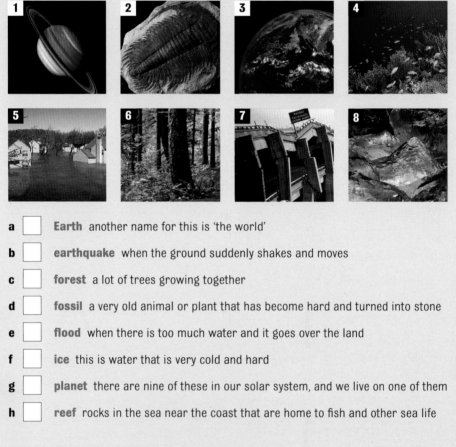

## BEFORE READING

**1 Match the pictures with the dictionary definitions below.**

**a** ☐  **Earth** another name for this is 'the world'

**b** ☐  **earthquake** when the ground suddenly shakes and moves

**c** ☐  **forest** a lot of trees growing together

**d** ☐  **fossil** a very old animal or plant that has become hard and turned into stone

**e** ☐  **flood** when there is too much water and it goes over the land

**f** ☐  **ice** this is water that is very cold and hard

**g** ☐  **planet** there are nine of these in our solar system, and we live on one of them

**h** ☐  **reef** rocks in the sea near the coast that are home to fish and other sea life

**2 What do you know about the Earth? Tick the boxes.**

**a** How much of the Earth has water on it?
   **1** ☐ more than 70%     **2** ☐ more than 90%

**b** Which part of the world has given us hundreds of medicines?
   **1** ☐ the seas     **2** ☐ the rainforests

**c** How many people are born in the world every minute?
   **1** ☐ 252     **2** ☐ 2,520

# Planet Earth

O n 28 February 2002, scientists in Kourou, French Guiana, were worried. They knew that in a few hours' time the Ariane **rocket** would leave on its journey. On the rocket was Envisat, the biggest and most expensive **satellite** ever made in Europe. Envisat was ready and waiting after twenty years' work by hundreds of people. But now, at the last minute, something was wrong with the rocket carrying the satellite.

**scientist** a person who studies the natural world

**rocket**

**Scientists** worked all night to get the rocket working again. Late in the evening on 1 March everyone in Kourou stopped working to watch the rocket leave. The weather was good and the rocket was ready. Five, four, three, two, one . . . the Ariane rocket went up into the sky, carrying Envisat with it.

*The Envisat satellite above Earth*

What is special about Envisat? It is as big as a bus, and very heavy. It travels 800 kilometres above the Earth, and it goes round the Earth once every 100 minutes. Envisat gets **power** from the light of the sun, and it uses that power to send **information** back to scientists on Earth. The information is about many different things, for example:

> ‣ changes in the ice in the Arctic and Antarctic
> ‣ the beginnings of floods and storms
> ‣ fires in forests
> ‣ early news of earthquakes
> ‣ information about the sea – how much food there is for fish, and where some water **plants** are a danger to life in the sea

They can use this information to make plans for the **future**, and also for the **present**. When the terrible storm **Cyclone** Nargis hit Myanmar in 2008, scientists got information about the floods from Envisat and sent it to Myanmar. Workers there used this information to get help to people who needed it. You can see pictures from Envisat at the ESA **website**.

One hundred and seventy years before Envisat left Kourou, another journey began – a journey that changed the way people think about life on Earth. On 31 December 1831, HMS *Beagle* left England on a five year journey to South America and the Pacific. On the *Beagle* was a young Englishman called Charles Darwin. Darwin was a clever young man from a rich English family. At first he **studied** to be a doctor, but then decided that he wanted to work for the church. He was also very interested in plants and animals, so when they asked him to travel on the *Beagle*, he said 'yes' – but he didn't get any money for his work on the ship. The *Beagle* spent five years travelling

**power** what makes something work

**information** facts

**plant** a small green thing, with leaves and, sometimes, flowers

**future** the time that will come

**present** today; now

**cyclone** a very strong tropical storm with strong winds that move in a circle

**website** a place on a computer where you can find information about people and businesses

**study** to learn

to **places** in South America and the Pacific, and Darwin looked carefully at the animals and plants in all these different places.

At this time, most scientists **believed** that **species** did not change. How did they explain fossils that were different from living species? They thought that from time to time a big change happened to the Earth, and then the old species died and new species took their place. So an old fossil and a new species could not come from the same family. But Darwin began to think that perhaps this was not true. In South America and in the Galapagos Islands, Darwin looked at some small birds called finches. He saw that the finches in the Galapagos Islands were not the same as the finches in South America; what is more, sometimes the finches of one island were different from the finches of another island. Finches that ate big **seeds** had big strong **bills**; finches that ate **insects** had narrow bills. Perhaps, Darwin thought, these birds were once the same, but because they lived in different places and ate different food they slowly changed. After he came back from his travels, Darwin spent a long time studying, reading, and writing about his **ideas**.

**place** a building, town, or country

**believe** to feel sure that something is true

**species** (*plural* **species**) a group of animals or plants that are the same in some way

**seeds** flowers and trees come from these

**insect** a small animal with six legs and a body that has three parts; ants and bees are insects

**idea** a plan or a new thought

bill

*Finches from the Galapagos Islands, 1835*

**kind** a type of thing; an apple is a kind of fruit

**chance** the possibility that something can happen

*More cats means better grass and fatter cows*

In the end, in 1858, Darwin's book *The Origin of Species* arrived in bookshops. All 1,250 books were sold on the first day. Darwin said in his book that any species could change over time into a new species. He also said that when something changed in a place – for example, when the weather changed, or when a new **kind** of food arrived – animals or plants that could learn to change too had the best **chance** of living through difficult times and doing well.

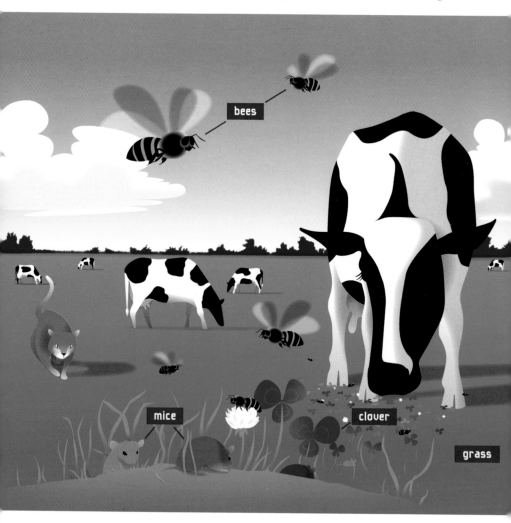

bees

mice

clover

grass

Many people were interested in Darwin's ideas. Some people agreed with them and some did not, but everyone began talking about the book, and some people got very angry about it.

Another idea of Darwin's was that English villages with a lot of old women had better **grass** and fatter cows. He explained it like this.

'Old women have more cats than most people. So more old women means more cats. Cats eat **mice**, and mice eat young **bees**. So more old women means more cats, fewer mice, and more bees. For good grass, you need **clover** – and for lots of clover, you need bees. So more old women means more cats, fewer mice, more bees, more clover, and better grass. And better grass means fatter cows. So in the end more old women means better grass and fatter cows.'

These days most people think that Darwin's ideas were right. Since Darwin's time we have learnt that animals, plants, people, and the **environment** are changing all the time; sometimes quickly, sometimes slowly, sometimes in good ways and sometimes in bad ways. We do not always know what those changes will be. Envisat can help us to see the changes that are happening to the Earth because of the things that people do, or because of storms, floods, or earthquakes.

Over the last fifty years, more and more people have begun to ask questions about what is happening in the environment. In 1992 people from 172 different countries met in Rio de Janeiro for the Earth **Summit**. For two weeks they talked about the dangers to the environment and agreed to find ways to make our planet a better place to live. In this book we will look at some famous people and **organizations** – like Greenpeace and WWF (World Wide Fund for Nature) – that have tried to make the Earth a better place.

**grass** it is green; gardens and fields have lots of it on the ground

**environment** everything around us: like the air, water, plants, animals

**summit** a meeting to talk about very important things

**organization** a group of people who work together to do something

## READING CHECK

**Choose the best words to finish the sentences.**

**a** Darwin was interested in . . .
  **1** ☑ plants and animals.   **2** ☐ planets and stars.   **3** ☐ ships and the sea.

**b** For his work on the *Beagle*, Darwin got . . .
  **1** ☐ a lot of money.   **2** ☐ a little money.   **3** ☐ no money at all.

**c** The *Beagle* travelled to . . .
  **1** ☐ North and South America.
  **2** ☐ South America and the Pacific.
  **3** ☐ Africa and India.

**d** Most scientists in the 1830s thought that . . .
  **1** ☐ an old species could slowly change into a new species.
  **2** ☐ an old species could quickly change into a new species.
  **3** ☐ an old species could not change into a new species.

**e** Darwin thought that the bills of finches changed because . . .
  **1** ☐ they ate different food.
  **2** ☐ they travelled around the world.
  **3** ☐ they were an old species.

**f** Darwin's book was called . . .
  **1** ☐ *The Beginning of Life*.
  **2** ☐ *The Origin of the Earth*.
  **3** ☐ *The Origin of Species*.

**g** When people began reading Darwin's book . . .
  **1** ☐ most people agreed with it.
  **2** ☐ everybody started talking about it.
  **3** ☐ people soon got bored with it.

**h** Darwin thought that English villages with lots of old women had . . .
  **1** ☐ fatter cats.   **2** ☐ fatter cows.   **3** ☐ more mice.

## WORD WORK

**Use the words from the Earth to complete the sentences.**

species
idea environment
chance power future
organization scientist
study plants summit
website information
kind

**a** Animals, trees, rivers, and mountains are all part of the
..environment.. .

**b** A . . . . . . . . . . . . . . . . . can get
. . . . . . . . . . . . . . . . . from fossils about
old animal or plant . . . . . . . . . . . . . . . . . .

**c** Every important . . . . . . . . . . . . . . . . . . . is
sending somebody to the . . . . . . . . . . . . . . . . . .
to talk about the world's problems.

**d** My computer stopped working last night because
there wasn't any . . . . . . . . . . . . . . . . . . .

**e** In the . . . . . . . . . . . . . . . . . perhaps people will . . . . . . . . . . . . . . . . . . the Earth from the
moon.

**f** If you want to find out about the floods in Asia, look on the internet. There must be a
. . . . . . . . . . . . . . . . . that can tell you about them.

**g** A pizza is a . . . . . . . . . . . . . . . . of food that you can make quickly.

**h** We need to decide where to go for our holiday – does anybody have a good
. . . . . . . . . . . . . . . . . ?

**i** If I have the . . . . . . . . . . . . . . . . . to visit New York, of course I'm going to go.

**j** I'd like a garden near my house that is full of green . . . . . . . . . . . . . . . . . . .

## GUESS WHAT

**Here are three people from the next chapter who
want to make the Earth a better place. What do
you know about them? Tick the boxes.**

|  | Rachel Carson | Leonardo DiCaprio | Sir Julian Huxley |
|---|---|---|---|
| **Who . . .** | | | |
| **a** . . . was a British scientist? | ☐ | ☐ | ☐ |
| **b** . . . is an American film star? | ☐ | ☐ | ☐ |
| **c** . . . was an American scientist? | ☐ | ☐ | ☐ |
| **d** . . . wrote a book called *Silent Spring*? | ☐ | ☐ | ☐ |
| **e** . . . has an organization that helps the environment? | ☐ | ☐ | ☐ |

7

# Going green

I n the early 1970s, the word 'green' began to **appear** everywhere. But this was not the colour green – it was a name for groups of people and **political** organizations. What does it mean to be green? Where does the name come from?

In the 1950s and 1960s, people began to use a lot of **pesticides** on plants and trees. Pesticides kill **insects** that eat vegetables and fruit; if the insects die, you get more vegetables and fruit, and you can make more money from them. Even today, the pesticide business makes three kilos of pesticides a year for every man, woman, and child on Earth. Where do all these pesticides go? Into the Earth, the rivers, the sea, the **air**, the birds, animals, and insects – and some of them go into your food.

Are pesticides good for you or bad for you? Does it matter? These questions worried a scientist called Rachel Carson. Rachel was born in 1907 in a quiet town by a river in Pennsylvania, in the United States. As a young child she was interested in living things, and when she got older she **became** a scientist. For a long time she worked for the American **government**. She wrote a book called *The Sea Around Us*, and lots of people read it and enjoyed it.

But her work taught her that everything – people, animals, birds, trees, rivers, the sea – is **part** of life; if we do something to one part, it may change another part. She decided to write another book about this, and in 1962 her book *Silent Spring* appeared. In this book she explained why she was worried about pesticides, especially when people use them over a long time. Millions of people read the book and began to think and

**appear** to be suddenly in front of someone's eyes

**political** of or about the work of government

**pesticide** something we use to kill the flies and other insects that damage plants

**air** the space above and around things; we take this in through our mouths and noses

**become** (*past* became, become) to begin to be

**government** the people who control a country

**part** some, but not all, of something

talk about these ideas, too.

What happens when you start using a lot of pesticides? Read this story about the cats with **parachutes** to find out.

parachutes

In Borneo in the 1950s, **mosquitoes** were giving people a disease called malaria. When people are ill with malaria, they feel hot, then cold, and very tired; sometimes they even die. So the government used a lot of pesticide called DDT to kill the mosquitoes. Soon there was less malaria – and that was a good thing. But then the grass **roofs** of people's houses started to fall on their heads. Why? Because **caterpillars** lived in the roofs and ate the grass. Before, **wasps** ate the caterpillars, but the DDT was killing the wasps, too. Now there was nothing to stop the caterpillars, and so the roofs started to fall down. Then there was a bigger **problem**. Cats

**problem**
something difficult

*Grass roofs in Borneo*

mosquitos

roof

wasp

caterpillar

rat

ate the animals that ate the wasps – and without food, the cats began to die. And when there were fewer cats, there were more rats. The **rats** made people ill, and so people were still dying. Now they had a worse problem than before because more people were dying because of the rats than from malaria – and that is why 14,000 cats arrived by parachute in the villages of Borneo in the 1950s!

**rubbish** things that you do not want any more

**protect** to keep someone or something from danger

**control** to make people or things do what you want

**wildlife** animals that are wild and live in a natural environment

**save** to take someone or something out of danger

**panda**

WWF symbol

WWF

sing pesticides was just one problem. After *Silent Spring* people began to talk about other world problems. How could we live in a world with more people and more **rubbish**, with dirty seas and dirty air? And then there were countries that were very, very rich, and countries that were terribly poor. For a lot of people that was a problem, too.

In the early 1970s the first political groups with green ideas appeared in Australia and New Zealand. The first political group that used the name 'green' was Die Grünen (the Greens) in Germany in the early 1980s.

What does it mean to be green? The most important thing for all greens is to **protect** the environment – the plants, the animals, the Earth, and the sea. Other important things for many greens are **controlling** the number of people on the Earth, and making life better for people without doing bad things to the environment.

WWF is an organization that works for the environment all over the world. It began when a group of scientists became worried about the **wildlife** in Africa. Sir Julian Huxley and other scientists visiting Africa in the 1960s saw that large numbers of animals were dying. They were afraid that the same problem was happening in other places in the world, too. When WWF began in 1961 its job was to **save** life on Earth by saving the environment. WWF used the picture of a **panda** as its **symbol**, because everybody knows this animal with big black eyes. Now

WWF is more than forty years old, and it uses its money to help save the environment and wildlife all over the world. WWF works to:

> ▸ save species that are in danger
> ▸ protect rivers and seas
> ▸ protect forests
> ▸ protect the environment from dangers like pesticides and changes in weather

Sometimes famous people talk about animals in danger, or problems with the environment. Are they really worried about wildlife, or do they just want to have their picture in the newspapers or on TV? It isn't always easy to know.

Leonardo DiCaprio is the famous film star who appeared in the films *Revolutionary Road*, *Romeo and Juliet*, and *Titanic*. He is interested in the environment and he has an organization called the Leonardo DiCaprio Foundation. The Foundation gives money to people who want to make the environment better. You can read about it on his website.

In 1999 he went to Thailand to be in the film *The Beach*. This film is about a number of young people who go to live on a beautiful beach, a long way from towns and people. The people making the film found the island of Ko Phi Phi Leh, which was very beautiful. They brought in a lot of trees which do not usually **grow** there and put them around the beach. When they finished the film they took away the trees and tried to make the beach the way it was before. But some people were very angry about the changes to Ko Phi Phi Leh. Perhaps it will be a long time before the beach is beautiful again.

Film stars come and go, but DiCaprio is still interested in the environment. In 2007 he made a film called *The 11th Hour*, about the problems of the environment today. 'The danger is now,' the film tells us.

**grow** (*past* **grew**, **grown**) to get bigger

## READING CHECK

**1 Put these sentences about Borneo in the 1950s in the correct order. Number them 1–7.**

**a** ☐ Mosquitoes died, and there was less malaria.

**b** ☐ The rats made people very ill.

**c** ☐ People were getting malaria from mosquitoes in Borneo in the 1950s.

**d** ☐ The government sent 14,000 cats to the villages by parachute.

**e** ☐ The government used DDT to kill the mosquitoes.

**f** ☐ The grass roofs of the houses started to fall down, and there were more rats.

**g** ☐ People began to die because of the rats, not because of malaria.

**2 Match the first and second parts of these sentences.**

**a** In the 1950s and 1960s . . .

**b** In 1961 . . .

**c** In 1962 . . .

**d** In the 1970s . . .

**e** In the 1980s . . .

**f** In 1999 . . .

**1** the first political groups with green ideas appeared.

**2** people started using pesticides.

**3** Leonardo DiCaprio went to Thailand to be in the film *The Beach*.

**4** Sir Julian Huxley and other scientists started WWF.

**5** Rachel Carson wrote *Silent Spring*.

**6** Die Grünen began in Germany.

## WORD WORK

Use the words on the beach to complete the sentences on page 13.

~~government~~   rubbish   save   problem   part   grow

# ACTIVITIES

**a** Every .government. in the world must think more about the environment.

**b** People in poor countries can't find food easily. It's a real ...................... for them.

**c** We must ...................... the number of pesticides people use. They use too many!

**d** Don't leave your ...................... in the countryside. Take it home with you.

**e** I arrived late, so I only saw ...................... of the film.

**f** We need to ...................... these pandas quickly or they will all die.

**g** My brother wants to ...................... a scientist when he is older.

**h** A lot of vegetables ...................... in my friend's garden.

**i** The island of Ko Phi Phi Leh ...................... in the film *The Beach*.

**j** We need to ...................... the world from people who want to destroy it.

**k** Die Grünen was a ...................... organization that started in Germany.

## GUESS WHAT

**The next chapter is about the organization called Greenpeace. What do you know about it? Tick the boxes.**   Yes   No

**a** A group of Canadian people started Greenpeace.  ☐ ☐

**b** Greenpeace is more than sixty years old.  ☐ ☐

**c** Greenpeace works to protect the environment.  ☐ ☐

**d** Greenpeace is a government organization.  ☐ ☐

**e** Greenpeace has had two ships called *Rainbow Warrior*.  ☐ ☐

**f** People from Greenpeace protest about the environment, but they do not fight.  ☐ ☐

control   protect   political   appears   become

# 3

# Greenpeace

**coast** the place where the land is next to the sea

**nuclear** a kind of power made from breaking atoms

**test** trying something new; to try something new

**protest** something that you do to say or show strongly that you do not like something; to say or show that you do not like something

**continue** to go on

**violence** when people use violence they fight or hurt other people

*Greenpeace protesters on the* Phyllis Cormack, *1971*

In September 1971, a group of twelve people left Vancouver, Canada, on an old fishing boat called the *Phyllis Cormack*. They were going to the island of Amchitka, off the west **coast** of Alaska. Amchitka was home to a lot of wildlife, but no people lived there. It was also in a part of the world where earthquakes often happen. The people on the *Phyllis Cormack* were worried because the United States was using Amchitka for **nuclear tests**. 'Perhaps they will not do their tests if we are staying on the island,' they thought. 'Perhaps other people will hear about our **protest** and tell the United States that they don't want the tests either.'

The United States did not stop the tests immediately, but this group of people **continued** to protest, and in 1972 the tests stopped. Then the group took a new name – Greenpeace. They wanted to make a world that was green, with no **violence** between people or countries. Now, over thirty years later, Greenpeace has offices in forty-one countries, and

nearly three million people all over the world belong to this organization. It does not make money, and it does not belong to any business or government. Most people know about Greenpeace because of their protests about things that are wrong. They make films, and talk on radio and TV, but they do not use violence. What kind of things does Greenpeace protest about? Here are some of them.

> **Whales**
Greenpeace has worked hard to protect whales and stop countries from **hunting** them.
> **Nuclear waste**
Many people in different countries around the world are worried about nuclear **waste**. Sometimes people put it in the sea; sometimes they put it under the ground; sometimes they pay poor countries to take nuclear waste. Greenpeace thinks this is dangerous.
> **Rainforests**
Greenpeace is fighting to save the trees in the rainforests of the world. Now a lot more people ask themselves, 'Where did this wood come from?' before they buy things made of wood. People want wood that does not come from the rainforests, because they know that the rainforests are in danger.

whale

**hunt** to look for and kill animals

**waste** the things you throw away because they are not useful; food that has passed through an animal

**rainforest** a forest where there is more than 254 centimetres of rain per year

**safe** not dangerous

**land** the part of the Earth that is not the sea

Greenpeace wants **safe** water, air, **land**, and food for everybody, and they know that we have to do things now before it is too late. When something happens at sea, Greenpeace goes there in a boat. The *Vega*, the *Greenpeace*, and the *Rainbow Warrior* are some of their boats. There have been two boats called *Rainbow Warrior*. In 1985 something happened to the first *Rainbow Warrior*, and people read about it all over the world.

# The Rainbow Warrior story

**damage** to break or harm something

**diver** someone who swims under the water

*The* Rainbow Warrior *could not sail again*

It was early in 1985. A young French woman called Frédérique Bonlieu was working in the Greenpeace office in Auckland, New Zealand. Frédérique sent letters to people and helped in the office. But her real name was Christine Cabon, and secretly she was working for the French government. Nobody knew that her real job was to get information about the *Rainbow Warrior*.

The French government was making plans to do some nuclear tests in the Pacific Ocean. Many people thought that was dangerous, and Greenpeace decided to send their ship *Rainbow Warrior* to the place where the French wanted to do the tests. Christine Cabon secretly sent information about the *Rainbow Warrior* to the French government. The French plan was to **damage** the ship and stop it sailing to the Pacific. After that, the nuclear tests could happen.

On 7 July 1985, the *Rainbow Warrior* arrived in Auckland. The ship looked very good, and a lot of people came to see it. Three days later, on the evening of 10 July, there was a birthday party on the ship. Around 8.30 p.m., while people enjoyed themselves on the ship, a French **diver** went quietly into the water and swam to the *Rainbow Warrior*. He put something onto the side of the ship in two places, and swam away again. Nobody on the ship saw or heard anything. Later, some of the people left the party to go for

a drink, but twelve people stayed on the ship.

Suddenly, at 11.38 p.m., there was a big **explosion** under the ship, and a hole as big as a car appeared in one side of it. Everyone had to hurry to leave the ship. Eleven people got off the ship, but one, a photographer called Fernando Pereira, went back to get his cameras. Then there was a second explosion. Pereira could not get off the ship, and he died there.

Soon the story was news all over the world. People in New Zealand and in many other countries helped the police with information. After a few days the New Zealand police found and took away two French people, Alain Mafart and Dominique Prieur. They were working for the French army, and they helped with the **attack** on the *Rainbow Warrior*.

At first the French government said that they knew nothing about the attack. But in September 1985, Prime Minister Laurent Fabius finally said that the divers attacked the ship after the French government told them to do it. Mafart and Prieur had to go to prison for ten years, but in fact they left after three years. France paid New Zealand seven million dollars because of the attack.

In August 1985 Greenpeace brought the *Rainbow Warrior* up from the bottom of the sea, but it could not sail again. What could they do with it? In the end, they took it to the Cavalli Islands, near the north of New Zealand's North Island. There they left the ship on the bottom of the sea. Now sea plants grow on the *Rainbow Warrior* and fish with bright colours swim in and out of her. You can go out on a boat and dive down to see the ship.

On 10 July 1989, exactly four years later, Greenpeace showed the world its new ship – *Rainbow Warrior II*. Now, when Greenpeace wants to protest about bad things that are happening all over the world, this new ship can take them there.

**explosion** when something breaks into pieces with a very loud noise

**attack** something that you do to fight someone; to start fighting someone

17

## READING CHECK

**Correct ten more mistakes in this summary of the *Rainbow Warrior* story.**

The ~~American~~ *French* government wanted to do some nuclear tests in the Atlantic Ocean. When

Greenpeace decided to send their plane *Rainbow Warrior* to protest about this, the French

made a plan to burn the ship. On 10 July there was a Christmas party on the ship. During

the party, a French diver walked to the *Rainbow Warrior*, put something on the top of the

ship and went away again. Later there were two explosions, and a sailor died. Two French

people went to hospital because of the attack, and France paid New Zealand seven hundred

dollars. Now the old *Rainbow Warrior* is on the bottom of the river near the Cavalli Islands,

and a new ship – *Rainbow Warrior II* – sails all over the world for Greenpeace.

## WORD WORK

**Complete the sentences on page 19 with words from the crossword.**

18

**a** France wanted to do some .... *nuclear* .... .... *tests* ..... in the Pacific.

**b** Greenpeace ................... about things that ................... the environment, but they never use ................... .

**c** Mafart and Prieur went to prison because of their ................... on the *Rainbow Warrior*.

**d** Greenpeace wants everyone to have water that is ................... to drink.

**e** It is very dangerous for the environment when factories throw away their ................... into the air, the sea, or rivers.

**f** The modern two-piece swimsuit for women got its name from a US nuclear ................... in a place called Bikini in 1946.

**g** In the Amazon ................... there are many animal and plant species that do not live in any other place in the world.

**h** Some people ................... animals and kill them as a sport.

**i** People often build new houses, roads and factories on ................... that was once a home for wild animals and plants.

**j** A ................... with lots of dirty beaches is bad for the holiday business, and it's bad for seabirds and animals, too.

## GUESS WHAT

**The next chapter is about tropical rainforests. What do you know about them?**

**Tick the boxes.**     **True**  **False**

**a** In tropical rainforests it rains all year round. ☐ ☐

**b** Trees in the rainforest can be 35 metres tall. ☐ ☐

**c** The rainforests help to clean our air. ☐ ☐

**d** There are more plant species in the forest of Ecuador than in all of Europe. ☐ ☐

**e** Cutting down rainforests is good for the environment. ☐ ☐

19

# 4

# Tropical rainforests

## What is a tropical rainforest?

**tropical** from the hottest part of the world

There are **tropical** rainforests in three parts of the world: Central and South America, West and Central Africa, and Southeast Asia and Australia. They are very wet; some get a lot of rain all year round, but some get rain only for a few months of the year. Tropical rainforests are in places that are near the hottest parts of the planet, so they are warm, too – usually between 20 °C and 35 °C.

At the highest part of the rainforest there are very tall trees, which grow up to thirty-five metres tall. Below them the tops of smaller trees come together like a roof of leaves. Here you find bright flowers and fruits, and many birds and animals come here to eat them. Below this there are smaller trees, and when you reach the ground it is dark, because the leaves of the trees stop a lot of the light from the sun.

**lemons**

**chocolate**

## What tropical rainforests give us

Tropical rainforests are rich in different species of trees, plants, insects, animals, and birds. For example, there are more than 15,000 plant species in the forests of Ecuador, but only 13,000 plant species in all of Europe.

**coconut**

**cola**

**Brazil nuts**

**sugar**

**vanilla**

Hundreds of different **medicines** have come from rainforest plants. And today we enjoy a lot of foods that came first from the rainforests or from places near them; for example, bananas, coffee, **coconut**, **vanilla**, **lemons**, **Brazil nuts**, tea, **sugar**, **chocolate**, and **cola**.

Every day when you wash your face or hair, **clean** your house, or drive your car, you are using things that come from the rainforest. And there are probably hundreds and hundreds of other useful things in the rainforests, too – we just don't know about them yet.

Rainforests help to give us clean air, too. Driving cars and burning wood makes the air dirty; trees take **carbon dioxide** from this dirty air and give us back **oxygen**.

## The strange story of the **golden toads**

People first saw the Monteverde golden toad in the 1960s in a rainforest in Costa Rica. They were a big surprise for the scientists who saw them. The **male** toads were only five centimetres long, and they were very bright orange. The **females** were a little bigger; they were black with **spots** of bright red and yellow.

Each year in April, during the time of the rains, male and female toads met in **pools** of water high up in the rainforest. They left their eggs in the pools, and the eggs soon grew into young toads. Then the toads disappeared into the rainforest for another year.

In 1988 scientists looked for the toads, but they only found ten, not hundreds. In 1989 they found one – but since then nobody has seen any golden toads.

What happened to the toads? Some say that changes in the weather killed the toads; others say that cutting down trees or using pesticides was the thing that killed them. Nobody really knows.

We do know that four species **disappear** every hour

**medicine** something you eat or drink to make you better when you are ill

**clean** to stop something being dirty; when something is no longer dirty

**carbon dioxide (CO₂)** something in the air from burning; animals breathe out carbon dioxide

**oxygen (O₂)** something in the air; animals need oxygen to live

**golden toad**

**male** an animal that cannot make eggs or have babies

**female** an animal that can make eggs and have babies

**spot** a circle of a different colour on something

**pool** a little water on the ground

**disappear** to go away suddenly

somewhere in the world because people are cutting down rainforests. Since this time yesterday, nearly one hundred species have disappeared – forever.

## The life and death of Chico Mendes

In 1925, Chico Mendes's family moved to west Brazil to work as **rubber** tappers. Rubber tappers make cuts in the rubber trees and get the rubber that comes out. In this way, they can sell the rubber and make money from the forest, without damaging the forest or the rubber trees.

Chico Mendes was born in Xapuri in 1944. His home was in the forest and at the age of nine he was tapping rubber like the rest of his family. He also looked for **nuts** and fruit in the forest and sold these things, too.

In the 1970s and 1980s, some new people became interested in the forest. They were Brazilian ranchers; they worked with **cattle** and they wanted the land for their animals. They began to buy large parts of the forest, then they cut down and burnt the trees. That of course meant the death of the forest – and no work or money for the rubber tappers. Chico got the rubber tappers together to fight for the forest. In 1985 he began an organization called the National Council of Rubber Tappers, bringing the workers together to protect their homes and their way of life.

Of course, there were people who did not agree with Chico. Some businesses and people from the government tried to stop him. At one time he went to prison, but he did not stop his fight. In 1988, Chico led rubber tappers from Xapuri to try and stop a rancher called Darly Alves da Silva. Darly Alves wanted to cut down the trees in one part of the forest, but it was the same part that the rubber tappers wanted to make into a **reserve**. The idea of the reserve was that the tappers could take rubber, nuts, and fruits from the forest, and at the same time they could protect it.

**rubber** something from a tree that we use to make things like balls and boots

**nut** the hard fruit of a tree or bush

**cattle** cows

**reserve** a place where animals and plants are safe

On 22 December 1988, Chico went to the door of his house. There he saw Darci Alves Pereira, the son of Darly Alves. The rancher shot Chico, and Chico died minutes later.

The death of Chico Mendes was news all over the world. Many people sent money to help the rubber tappers try to save the rainforest. In 1990 Darly Alves da Silva and Darci Alves Pereira went to prison for nineteen years. They escaped in 1993, but the police found them in 1996 and sent them back to prison.

*Rubber tapping in the Amazon*

Now in Brazil there is a reserve in the rainforest that has Chico Mendes's name. And Brazil remembered Chico Mendes when it decided to be the place for the Earth Summit in 1992.

*Chico Mendes at home, November 1988*

## READING CHECK

**Are these sentences true or false? Tick the boxes.**

| | | True | False |
|---|---|:---:|:---:|
| a | Rubber tappers cut down trees to get rubber. | ☐ | ☑ |
| b | Chico Mendes lived in the forest with his family. | ☐ | ☐ |
| c | Brazilian ranchers cut down and burned the trees because they wanted land for houses. | ☐ | ☐ |
| d | Chico started his organization to help the rubber tappers and protect the forest. | ☐ | ☐ |
| e | Chico wanted to protect the forest, but Darly Alves da Silva wanted to cut part of it down. | ☐ | ☐ |
| f | Darci Alves Pereira shot Chico Mendes at his father's house. | ☐ | ☐ |
| g | Darly Alves da Silva and Darci Alves Periera had to pay a lot of money because they shot Chico. | ☐ | ☐ |
| h | Now there is a Chico Mendes reserve in the Brazilian rainforest. | ☐ | ☐ |

## WORD WORK

**Use the words in the rainforest to complete the sentences.**

male   tropical   medicine   carbon dioxide   female   pools   disappear   rubber   cattle   reserve   oxygen

a   Many species of plants and animals ...disappear.. from the world every day, and once they've gone, we won't be able to get them back.

b   When you are ill, .................. can help to make you better.

24

c The ................ golden toad is only five centimetres long; and the
  ................ golden toad is a little bigger, and she has bright red and yellow
  spots.

d Ranchers need a lot of land, because their ................ need a lot of grass
  to eat.

e Animals in the rainforest go to ................ to get water to drink.

f In ................ places it is always warm and often wet.

g Trees are very important for life on Earth, because they take in ................
  ................ from the dirty air, and give out ................ .

h If you want your feet to stay dry in wet weather, you need to get some .
  ................ boots.

i Animals and plants are safe in a ................ , because people can't hunt or
  cut things down there.

## GUESS WHAT

**The next chapter is about safe places for animals. What do you think are the
correct answers to these questions?**

a What was the number of bison in North America in the early 1800s?

  **1** ☐ 60 million    **2** ☐ 100 million    **3** ☐ 120 million

b What was the number of bison in North America In 1895?

  **1** ☐ 200    **2** ☐ 800    **3** ☐ 1,500

c What is the number of bison in North America today?

  **1** ☐ 50,000    **2** ☐ 150,000    **3** ☐ 350,000

d Which country has a park to protect jaguars?

  **1** ☐ Belize    **2** ☐ Chile    **3** ☐ Mexico

e What percentage of the world's land is now national parks?

  **1** ☐ 1%    **2** ☐ 3%    **3** ☐ 5%

bison

jaguar

YELLOWSTONE NATIONAL PARK

national park

## 5

# Creating safe places

People need **space** to live, work, and play, and animals need space too. Sometimes it is difficult to find space for both people and animals.

To begin with, just think about the changes in the number of people on the Earth. In the year 1100 there were 320 million people on the planet. In the next eight hundred years the number of people slowly grew to 1,500 million (1.5 **billion**). But since 1900 the number of people has grown more quickly: 2.5 billion in 1950, 5 billion in 1987, and 6.6 billion in 2008. By 2050 how many people will there be?

Every year there are more and more people on the Earth. They cut down trees and take land for their cattle, sheep and other animals, or to grow food, or to build houses and cities. That means less space for the wild animals of the forest and open land. What happens when people and animals try to live next to one another?

**space** a place that is big enough

**billion** one thousand million

**horn**

**Native American** a person who lived in America before white people arrived

**skin** what is on the outside of an animal's body

**canoe** a long narrow boat

**bone** a hard white thing inside an animal's body

## The North American bison

The first bison came to North America from Asia about 200,000 years ago. They were very big, heavy animals – about 2,300 kilograms – with **horns** nearly two metres across.

The **Native Americans** began to hunt bison thousands of years ago. They used the **skins** to make clothes, homes, and **canoes**, and from the **bones** they made things to fight with. The bison was a very important part of their lives. In the early 1800s there were about 60 million bison across all of North America.

When Europeans came to North America they too were

interested in the bison. They enjoyed hunting and wanted **national park**
a large piece of
beautiful land that
the government
looks after the skins to make coats, so they began to kill bison by the million. Often they took the skins and some of the meat from the head, and left the rest of the animal there on the ground. White people also killed bison because they thought they were a danger to their cattle. You could even pay ten dollars to ride on a train and shoot bison all day.

By 1895, there were only 800 bison in North America. In 1902 people took forty-one animals to Yellowstone **National Park**. Nobody can hunt animals in a national park, so the bison could live there without danger. Now there are about 350,000 bison in North America again. That is very lucky. When there are only 800 animals of one species in the world, it is very easy for the species to disappear forever.

You can find national parks in different parts of the world. In Australia there is one around the Great Barrier Reef, which protects the fish and plants that live there. Some parks are made to protect places that are beautiful, like Yosemite Park in the United States, or Sagarmatha National Park in Nepal. But how did national parks begin? The first national park was made in the United States more than a hundred years ago, and the person who worked hardest to make it was John Muir.

*The Great Barrier Reef is a national park*

John Muir
in Yosemite
National Park,
1903

## John Muir

Muir was born in Scotland in 1838, but moved to the United States with his family in 1849. He worked for his father, looking after his animals and growing food, but he also enjoyed walking in the forests and fields near his home. In 1863 he began travelling across the United States and Canada, and went to many other parts of the world, too. In 1868 he arrived in California. When he saw the beautiful mountains of the Sierra Nevada for the first time, he thought that they were wonderful, and from that time California was his home. He went on travelling and writing, telling people about the mountains and the wild country, and asking them to enjoy and protect these special places.

Animals like sheep and cattle damaged the mountain forests, and this worried Muir. He wrote to newspapers and gave talks about the problem. At last, in 1890, the US government made Yosemite National Park. Muir helped to make four more national parks, and he began the Sierra Club to help protect wild places. He also wrote many books about national parks and wild places, and people called him 'the father of the national parks'. He went on doing this work until he died in 1914.

The idea of national parks travelled to other countries and today nearly 3% of the world's land is safe. But some animals are alive today mostly because one person has worked very hard to make a safe place for them. What makes somebody decide to do this?

## Alan Rabinowitz

It is not unusual for children to like animals, but Alan Rabinowitz had a special **reason** for this. When he was a child, he couldn't talk very well, and he did not like speaking. It was easier for him to **communicate** with animals than with people, and he spent a lot of time with animals. When he was older he was still interested in animals, and he studied them at university. Then in 1979 he got a job in Belize, in Central America. His job was to study **jaguars**.

**reason** why you do something

**communicate** to send a message from one person to another

jaguar

Rabinowitz's plan was to catch jaguars and put radios on them. Then he could learn about how they lived and what dangers there were for jaguars in Belize. He was the first person to study jaguars like this. He spent three years in Belize doing this; during this time he was in a plane crash, and a wild animal killed one of his workers, but he still went on working.

After five years, in 1984, Rabinowitz knew a lot about jaguars. He talked to the government of Belize, and they agreed to make a park, called Cockscomb Wildlife Sanctuary, where the animals would be safe. Now, Cockscomb is the biggest forest that is safe for animals in all of Central America.

Once the people of Belize killed the jaguars; now they protect them. People come from other countries to see the jaguars, and that brings money to Belize.

Now Rabinowitz writes books and helps to run Panthera, an organization which works to save the big wild cats of the world. But he still works with animals as often as he can.

*Alan Rabinowitz*

## READING CHECK

**Match the first and second parts of these sentences.**

**a** Native Americans . . .

**b** White hunters . . .

**c** John Muir . . .

**d** The US government . . .

**e** Alan Rabinowitz . . .

**f** The government of Belize . . .

**1** was called 'the father of the national parks'.

**2** studied jaguars in Belize for five years.

**3** killed millions of bison for sport in the 1800s.

**4** used the skins of bison to make clothes, homes and canoes.

**5** made the biggest park where animals can be safe in the whole of Central America.

**6** made Yosemite National Park in 1890.

## WORD WORK

**Match the words in the mountains with the definitions.**

national park    communicate
space
reason          Native American
skin        bone
billion

**a** Native American ......................... one of the first people who lived in North America

**b** ......................... why you do something

**c** ......................... a place that is big enough to do something

**d** ......................... to send a message from one person to another

**e** ......................... a large piece of beautiful land that the government looks after

**f** ......................... what is on the outside of an animal's body

**g** ......................... one thousand million

**h** ......................... a hard white thing inside an animal's body

# ACTIVITIES

## GUESS WHAT

**The next chapter is about the sea. Tick the boxes to complete the sentences.**

Emperor penguin

Polar bear

**a** The deepest part of the ocean is more than . . . . . . kilometres deep.

   **1** ☐ 10         **2** ☐ 50         **3** ☐ 100

**b** There are . . . . . . species of penguin in the world.

   **1** ☐ 8         **2** ☐ 18         **3** ☐ 28

**c** Emperor penguins can stay under water for as long as . . . . . . minutes.

   **1** ☐ 11         **2** ☐ 15         **3** ☐ 21

**d** Polar bears live in the . . . . . . .

   **1** ☐ Arctic         **2** ☐ Antarctic         **3** ☐ Pacific

**e** Dolphins can live for as long as . . . . . . years.

   **1** ☐ 60         **2** ☐ 50         **3** ☐ 40

dolphins

# 6

# The oceans

I f you go high up into the air and look at the Earth, the colour you will see most is blue. There is water on 361 million square kilometres of our planet – that is more than 70% of the Earth. In many places the world's **oceans** are 5,000 metres deep. The deepest part of the ocean is the Mariana Trench, east of the Philippines, which goes down for 10.9 kilometres. In the warmest places, the water in the oceans can be 26 °C, but in the icy waters near Antarctica it can be as cold as –1.4 °C. And there are hundreds of different species in the sea, from very little ones up to the blue whale, which can grow to twenty-six metres long.

## Birds that cannot fly

'They swam like fish, and made a noise like a wild horse. They were birds that could not fly – but they jumped out of the water.' What were these strange things? In 1498, the Portuguese traveller Vasco da Gama was surprised to see these animals in the Atlantic Ocean, far from land. They were penguins, and they are still some of the most interesting and **popular** animals of the ocean.

There are eighteen species of penguin in the world today. Two species – the Adélie and the Emperor penguins – live in Antarctica, but the others live in the southern oceans, and they spend most of their time (sometimes as much as 80% of it) in the sea. All penguins have black backs and white fronts; this helps to protect them when they are in the water, because it is difficult to see them from above or from below. They do not have the same wings and **tails** as birds that fly in the air; they have little short wings and tails, and big feet which help them

**ocean** a large sea

**popular** something or someone that lots of people like is popular

**tail** the long thing at the back of an animal's body

to 'fly' in the water. But different species have different colours **dive** to swim under water on their heads, and penguins can be as small as a chicken or as big as a small child.

It is often funny to watch penguins on land because their bodies look fat and uncomfortable. But in the water it is very different. Penguins stopped flying and began to live in the water about fifty million years ago, and their bodies have slowly changed. Now the water moves easily over their bodies, and this means they can travel very fast; as much as twenty-four kilometres per hour. They can also travel a long way. Emperor penguins, for example, can stay at sea for a month and travel almost 1,600 kilometres.

They are very good at **diving**, too. Scientists have studied Emperor penguins, and these birds can stay under water for as much as eleven minutes at a time, and can dive down 540 metres. Penguin eyes can see very well, both in the air and in the water, and they have heavy bones that help them to dive down deep.

## Danger for penguins

Penguins are not usually afraid of people. In fact, they are often interested in people and will come to see what they are *Adélie penguins like it cold*

doing. Because of this it has been easy in the past for people to take their eggs or even to catch them. For example, in 1867 in the Falkland Islands (las Islas Malvinas) people killed 405,000 penguins to get the **oil** from their bodies. The birds nearly disappeared from the islands.

Today there are different dangers for penguins. One problem is that they have lost some of the places where they usually leave their eggs. Another danger is that animals like rats and dogs eat the eggs and young birds. But scientists are now worried about a new problem – changes in the weather. Warmer seas mean less food for the penguins, and so their numbers are becoming smaller. This is the biggest problem for penguins that live in the coldest places, like Emperor penguins. Emperor penguins can stay alive when it is as cold as –60 °C. We must hope that warmer weather does not mean the end for these surprising birds.

## Big bears

It is not only penguins that are in danger from changes to the weather. Polar bears are in trouble too.

There have been polar bears in the Arctic for thousands of years. They are often 2 metres tall or more, and as heavy as 300 kilos. Their big feet help them to walk across snow and ice, and they are very good swimmers too. The most important food for polar bears is **seals**. The bears wait quietly near holes in the ice where the seals come up. When they can smell a seal, they pull it out of the water, kill it and eat it. If they eat a lot of seals in the winter months, they can live with little or no food in summer.

But things are changing. The Arctic ice is **melting** earlier in the spring now – perhaps three weeks earlier – so the bears have less time to hunt for, and eat seals. Then in the autumn the hungry bears have to wait longer before they can swim back to the ice. Today's bears are thinner, and they are not as

**oil** a thick liquid from plants or animals, often used for cooking; a black liquid that comes from the ground and is used to make power

**seal** an animal that lives in cold seas

**melt** to change from ice to water

heavy. In just twenty years the number of polar bears has gone from about 32,000 to 25,000.

Why is the ice melting? Global warming – which means a change to warmer weather all over the world – is happening everywhere. People drive cars, travel in planes, burn forests, and keep animals – and all of these things help to change our weather. So scientists say that in a hundred years from now perhaps there will be no more polar bears in the world.

## Little fish

Do you remember the film *Finding Nemo?* In 2003 millions of people watched and enjoyed the story of the little fish and his father who loses him and then finds him again.

It is not surprising that after they saw the film a lot of people – many of them children – wanted a fish like Nemo. Nemo was a clownfish, a little orange and white fish that lives in warm waters near Australia and the Philippines.

What happened next? It is possible to **breed** clownfish and sell them, but it isn't always easy. One problem is that clownfish are not good parents – they often eat the baby fish! So people caught wild fish and took them to the USA and other countries to sell them. And so the numbers of wild fish got smaller and smaller.

Now scientists in the USA are working to make breeding the fish easier. But some people say that there is a better answer to this problem: Leave Nemo in the ocean, where he belongs!

**breed** to keep animals so that they will produce baby animals

35

## Everybody's favourite

In the last few years, swimming with dolphins has become very popular. But people have always liked dolphins. There are books, songs, and films about them, and people put pictures of them on their walls, their clothes, and their websites. Dolphins live together in small groups, and they can live for as long as forty years. Like penguins, they can swim very fast and dive very deep, but they can also jump very high out of the water. To find their food they send sounds through the water and listen to the sounds that come back. They also communicate with one another, and some people think that each dolphin has its own special sound.

tuna in a tin

For many years fishermen have known that dolphins and **tuna** often travel together. If you want to catch tuna, you look for dolphins. This was not a problem until 1959, when a new kind of fishing boat appeared.

helicopter

Near the coast of California in the United States you can see a very big kind of fishing boat, which is more than sixty metres long. It sends a **helicopter** out to look for dolphins. When it finds them, the helicopter goes down near to the water. The dolphins, and the tuna fish that are with them, are afraid of the helicopter and they swim away from it – but

*Tuna fishing can kill dolphins too*

in front of them is the boat. When they are near the boat, the fishermen pull a big **net** around the dolphins and tuna, and close it like a big bag. The net is 1.6 kilometres long, and more than 100 metres deep. They pull the net onto the boat, drop the dolphins back into the water, and the tuna stay on the boat. But this often hurts or kills the dolphins. These big boats have killed at least seven million dolphins since the 1960s.

In the 1960s about 350,000 dolphins died this way every year. Then there were new **laws** about **tins** of tuna. The tins had to show if the tuna came from a 'dolphin-friendly' fishing boat – a boat that does not kill dolphins. In 1986, the number of dolphins that died was 133,000, and in 2001 about 2,027. But is this the real number? We don't really know. Perhaps it is much more than this. The big fishing boats now have to carry somebody who watches and counts the number of dead dolphins – but they can also tell the fishermen to 'lose' the dead dolphins before anyone sees them. Some dolphins die while the helicopter is following them, and baby dolphins may die if their mothers are killed.

**net** something like a big bag that you use to catch fish

**law** something that tells you what you must or must not do

**tin** a metal box for food or drink

What can you do?
▸ Look for tins of tuna with 'dolphin-friendly' on the label. Find out what that means. Can they show that they do not kill dolphins when they catch tuna? Write to them or look at their website.
▸ Organizations like Greenpeace, Defenders of Wildlife, and Friends of the Earth have lots of information about dolphins, and they have ideas about what you can do to help protect them. Write to them or look at their websites.
▸ Stop eating tuna! Or if you really like tuna, make sure that you only eat tins of 'dolphin-friendly' tuna.

## READING CHECK

**1 Correct the mistakes in these sentences about penguins and dolphins.**

Two

**a** ~~Eighteen~~ species of penguin live in Antarctica.

**b** Penguins have big wings that help them to 'fly' in the water.

**c** Penguins stopped singing about fifty million years ago.

**d** Emperor penguins can stay at sea for a year.

**e** Penguins have heavy heads that help them dive down deep.

**f** Penguins are usually afraid of people.

**g** Dolphins live together in big groups.

**h** Dolphins find their food by smell.

**i** 'Dolphin-friendly' means something that hurts dolphins.

**j** Fisherman catching whales often kill dolphins.

**2 Match the first and second parts of these sentences.**

**a** Polar bears live . . .

**b** Polar bears can move easily on snow and ice . . .

**c** The Arctic ice is melting . . .

**d** Clownfish live . . .

**e** Lots of people like clownfish . . .

**f** People caught wild clownfish and took them to the USA . . .

**1** because of global warming.

**2** in the land and water of the Arctic.

**3** because people there wanted to buy them for their children.

**4** because they have big feet.

**5** in the warm seas near Australia and the Philippines.

**6** because they enjoyed the film *Finding Nemo*.

## WORD WORK

**Complete the crossword puzzle with words from Chapter 6.**

**a** a large animal that polar bears eat

**b** to keep animals to get more baby animals

**c** to change from ice to water

**d** a metal box for food or drink

**e** a large sea

**f** a thick liquid that comes from plants or animals

**g** something that lots of people like is this

## GUESS WHAT

**In the next chapter you will read about the accident that happened in Chernobyl. What do you know about it? Tick the boxes.**

| | Yes | No |
|---|---|---|
| **a** Chernobyl was a town in the Ukraine. | ☐ | ☐ |
| **b** Nuclear power was made here. | ☐ | ☐ |
| **c** The accident happened in 1989. | ☐ | ☐ |
| **d** Chernobyl is a safe place to visit now. | ☐ | ☐ |
| **e** No one died in the accident. | ☐ | ☐ |
| **f** Thousands of people had to leave their homes here. | ☐ | ☐ |

*The power plant at Chernobyl after the explosion*

# 7
# Cleaning up

**machine** something that does work for people

**tanker** a very large ship that carries oil

**captain** the most important person on a ship

**disaster** something very bad that happens and that may hurt or kill a lot of people

We can't live without oil – cars, trains, planes, and **machines** all use oil. But we can only find oil in some parts of the world, and we use **tankers** to carry the oil across the oceans to the countries that need it. The tankers have become bigger and bigger – so when there is an accident sometimes millions of litres of oil go into the sea, or onto the coast. One of the most famous of these accidents was in 1989, in a lonely part of Alaska.

## Exxon Valdez

At 9 p.m. on the night of 23 March 1989, the *Exxon Valdez* began to sail south from Valdez in Alaska. There was ice in the sea, so the **captain** told the sailors to sail to one side. He told them to sail straight on in the usual way when they were past the ice. But, for some reason, they didn't do this, and just after midnight the *Exxon Valdez* hit Bligh Reef.

**Disaster!** Forty million litres of oil came out of the *Exxon Valdez*. That is about enough to fill 125 twenty-five-metre swimming pools. Over the next eight weeks the oil went along the coast, and in the end it arrived at the village of Chignik – 740 kilometres from Bligh Reef. But because there are so many little islands in this part of Alaska, there was oil on 2,240 kilometres of coast.

How many died? 250,000 sea birds, 2,800 sea **otters**, 300 seals, 250 bald **eagles**, 22 **killer whales**, and millions of fish eggs.

This wasn't the biggest oil

eagle

killer whale

otter

40

disaster in the world, but it was certainly one of the worst. Cleaning the beaches was difficult: 10,000 people, 1,000 boats, and 100 planes and helicopters helped in this long job. But even today some beaches still have oil on them.

*Forty million litres of oil came out of the Exxon Valdez*

The Exxon oil **company** spent about 2.1 billion dollars on the job of cleaning the beaches. But many scientists now think that sea water hitting the beaches wildly during winter storms did most of the cleaning.

After the accident the *Exxon Valdez* got a new name; *Sea River Mediterranean*. It still carries oil across the Atlantic, but the **law** says it can never go back to Alaska.

What has changed? Now, when tankers leave Valdez full of oil, two boats go with them. They can help if there is a problem. There are also lots of machines ready to take away the oil after an accident. They can take 46,500,000 litres of oil off the top of the water in seventy-two hours. And every year people **practise** what to do if there is another oil tanker disaster. Nobody wants another accident in Alaska like the *Exxon Valdez*, but if an accident does happen, they will be ready to stop so much oil going onto the beaches, and killing birds and sea animals.

**company** a group of people who work in the same business

**law** a rule of a country that says what you can and cannot do

**practise** to do something many times so that you can do it well

## Chenega Bay

**wave** a line of water that moves across the top of the sea

**destroy** to break every part of something or someone

It took just a few hours for the oil from the *Exxon Valdez* to get to Chenega Bay, a small Alaskan village with just forty-eight people. And this wasn't the first disaster in their lives.

In 1964 there was a terrible earthquake in Alaska, and two very big **waves destroyed** the village and killed twenty-three people. After eighteen years the people of Chenega Bay came together and built a new village. That was in 1982. Just seven years later came the day that people in Chenega Bay call 'the day the water died'.

Before the *Exxon Valdez* disaster people in Chenega Bay got a lot of their food from the sea. Now there is less food and some of it is less safe. A lot of people come to visit this part of Alaska now. They bring money, but they bring noise and rubbish, too. Not everybody is happy about that.

Some people left the village to go and work in Valdez, and some people used the money that the Exxon company paid them after the disaster to move away from Chenega Bay. But a number of people have stayed, and they are teaching their children to know about and protect their environment. They

*Cleaning up the oil on the coast of Alaska, 1989*

have lived through one disaster, they say, and they can live through another.

## Chernobyl

When scientists first made plans for nuclear **power plants**, a lot of people thought that this would be the best way to make **electricity** in the future. It was clean and safe, and it did not make big changes in the land around the power plant. Later people began to see that it was not so easy. Nuclear power plants could be very dangerous places, and governments had to spend millions of dollars to make them safe.

Before April 1986, not many people outside the Ukraine knew anything about the town called Chernobyl. But since that time it has become a name that millions of people know. On 26 April 1986, there was a terrible nuclear accident at Chernobyl.

On that night, a test at the nuclear power plant went wrong. Part of the power plant got very hot, and there was a big explosion. **Radioactive material** went out of the power plant and up into the air, and it travelled across northern Europe.

Thirty-one people died at the time of the accident, but many more died later because the radioactive material made them ill. Some of them were people who helped to clean up after the accident. How many people have died because of Chernobyl? Perhaps thousands, perhaps tens of thousands – we can't be sure. But it is sure that many more people will die in the future because of problems that began at the time of the disaster. More and more people are becoming ill, especially with **cancer**. Many people had to leave their homes – 116,000 after the accident, and another 210,000 people between 1990 and 1995. Many people feel worried and afraid about what will happen to them in the future.

**power plant** a building where electricity is made

**electricity** power that comes along wires and makes things work; computers and TVs use electricity

**radioactive material** something dangerous that you find in a nuclear power plant

**cancer** cancer makes people very ill, and can often kill them

*The land around Chernobyl is still radioactive*

adezhda Nikolaevna Timoshenko lived in the village of Borshchyovka from 1969 to 1986. This village was just twelve kilometres from Chernobyl. This is her story about what happened that day and afterwards.

'It was a very warm and sunny day. We could hear some birds singing in the sky. We had no idea about the terrible disaster. We found out what happened only early in the evening. A friend's son came to our village in a car with a radio. So we heard about the disaster on this radio.

'The people in our village did not **panic** at all. They gave us special medicine. Suddenly it started raining. I was outside in this rain. Next morning I saw some strange red spots on my skin. I was afraid, and then they told me that the rain was radioactive, and the red spots on my face would disappear soon. It was some time before the spots went away.

'They took us away from the village on 4 May. The children left the week before. Six buses arrived at the village to take

**panic** to do things without thinking carefully because you are frightened

people away. We could take only a few things with us that we needed to live.

'They took us to a village called Babchino. Those who had nowhere to go stayed in this village, in an old school. In about the middle of May they told us that we could not go home – the land was too radioactive. We got some money for our homes and other things of ours. It was not big money. But it was enough to buy some things for a new flat that was now our home in Igovka.

'We once visited our old home. You know, remembering the past now makes me shake. When we came to see our village, we could not find the birds or gardens that were there before. When I came into my house I did not find any of the things that were there before.

'Once the place was beautiful, there were forests, fields and the Pripyat River. Many people came to enjoy it. Now it is all different, everything has changed. We can visit the place only twice a year – on 9 May, and on a holiday called *Radovnitsa*. Chernobyl was a disaster. For me it is hard to forget, and terrible to remember.'

What has changed? Chernobyl is still a very dangerous place. Russia, the Ukraine, and a number of European countries are working together to make a giant **cover** to put over the power plant. Then the radioactive material will stay inside.

In a lot of countries people have begun to use new ways of making electricity – from wind, for example, or from the power of the sea. These are both clean and safe for the environment. But countries like China, India, and Russia are planning and building new nuclear power plants. Will these be safe? Have we learnt our lessons? Or is there a new Chernobyl disaster waiting for us in the future?

**cover** this goes on top of something

## READING CHECK

**Choose the correct words to complete these sentences.**

**a** The *Exxon Valdez* hit (Bligh Reef)  ice in the sea   Chenega bay .

**b** The Exxon oil company spent about   2.1   3.1   4.1   billion dollars cleaning the beaches.

**c** The *Exxon Valdez* still carries oil across the   Pacific   Atlantic   Mediterranean .

**d** Hundreds of   seals   penguins   dolphins   died from the *Exxon Valdez* oil.

**e** In 1964 there was a terrible   earthquake   explosion   nuclear accident   in Chenega Bay.

**f** The day of the Chernobyl disaster was   dry and cold   warm and sunny   cold and wet .

**g** People in Borshchyovka learned about Chernobyl from the   newspaper   TV   radio .

**h** People from the village stayed in an old   school   hospital   station   in Babchino.

**i** Nadezhda Timoshenko found   black   red   white   spots on her skin.

**j** Nadezhda got some   land   buildings   money   to help her make a new home.

## WORD WORK

**Complete the words to make sentences. All the words come from Chapter 7.**

**a** Before 1986, Chernobyl was just another **p o w e r   p l a n t**, making **e _ _ c t _ i _ _ t y** for the Ukraine.

**b** If you work with **r _ d _ _ a _ t _ v _   m _ t _ _ i _ l**, it is possible that you will get **c _ n _ _ r**.

**c** When the **t _ n _ _ r** called the *Exxon Valdez* left Valdez one night, the **c _ p _ _ i _** told the sailors to stay away from the ice.

**d** The Exxon oil **c _ m _ _ n _** spent billions of dollars getting the oil off the beaches.

**e** The *Exxon Valdez* was a **d _ s _ s _ _ r** for thousands of birds, animals, and fish in Alaska.

**f** Today in Valdez, there are lots of **m a _ _ _ n _ s** that can clean in the water if there is an accident.

**g** After an earthquake, very big waves can _ e s _ _ o _ roads and buildings.

**h** When an accident happens, it can be hard to think clearly and not **p** _ _ **i** _ .

**i** If you want to do something well, you must _ **r** _ **c** _ _ **s** _ it again and again.

## GUESS WHAT

**The next chapter is about making a better world for the future.**
**Which of these ideas will you find there? Tick the boxes.**  **Yes**  **No**

**a** We need to put less carbon dioxide into the atmosphere.  ☐ ☐

**b** We need to travel by plane, not by bicycle.  ☐ ☐

**c** We need to eat a lot of meat.  ☐ ☐

**d** We need to drive small cars, not big ones.  ☐ ☐

**e** We need to buy water in bottles.  ☐ ☐

**f** We need to buy power made from the wind or sea.  ☐ ☐

# A green future?

## 8

**W**hat can we do to protect our environment? How can we make a green future for the world? People have talked about these questions a lot, and they have spent a lot of money trying to find answers.

Many people think that global warming is one of the biggest problems – and not just for polar bears. If the weather gets warmer, there will be lots of changes, and a lot of them will not be good. One of the reasons for global warming is that people put carbon dioxide into the **atmosphere**.

The air that comes out of our mouths has carbon dioxide in it. When we drive cars or travel on planes and trains, they put carbon dioxide into the atmosphere too. Burn oil to make your house warm, and that's more carbon dioxide. But we need to breathe, eat, travel, and have warm houses when it's cold – so what can we do?

**atmosphere** the mixture of gases around the Earth

**carbon footprint** the amount of carbon that one person puts into the atmosphere

## Carbon footprint

When you walk across a floor with wet feet, you can see a line of 'feet' behind you. Those are your footprints. In the same way, people leave behind a **carbon footprint** that shows how much carbon dioxide they make in their lives. If you travel by car and buy lots of new things, you have a bigger carbon footprint. If you walk and buy

**second-hand** things, you have a smaller carbon footprint. These are some of the things that make a carbon footprint smaller or bigger.

**second-hand**
used by another
person before

| ▸ Smaller | ▸ Bigger |
|---|---|
| eat no meat | eat lots of meat |
| eat food that grows nearby | eat food from far away |
| buy clothes and other things that are second-hand | always buy new clothes |
| walk or ride a bicycle | travel a lot |
| drive a small car | drive a large car |

Anyone can find out their carbon footprint. A lot of websites can help you to do it. You answer questions about your house, your car, and the food that you eat, and the website will tell you your carbon footprint.

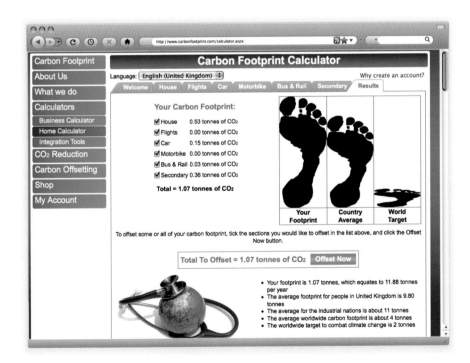

**solve** to find the answer to a problem

Now you know your carbon footprint, how can you make it smaller? Here are some ideas.

> ‣ Don't take the car – walk or ride a bicycle when you can.
> ‣ Turn off the light when you leave a room.
> ‣ Turn off computers, TVs etc when you are not using them.
> ‣ Buy food from places close to your home. Or grow vegetables and fruit yourself!
> ‣ Don't buy too many new clothes. Don't throw your old clothes away – sell them, or take them to second-hand shops.
> ‣ Try cooking meals with only a little meat, or no meat at all.
> ‣ Don't buy water in bottles.
> ‣ Buy power made from the wind or sea if you can.
> ‣ Think before you buy things.

These are small things, but if everyone makes small changes like these, it will help the environment.

## Earth Summit 2002

On 26 August 2002, ten years after the Rio Summit, 60,000 people came to Johannesburg in South Africa for another Earth Summit. Some of them were important people from the governments of different countries, but President Bush of the United States did not come.

Many governments are now working hard to **solve** problems in the environment. In Denmark, for example, 18% of the country's electricity comes from power plants that use the power of the wind. But a lot of people think that rich countries, like America, could do more to help with these problems.

In Johannesburg the Summit agreed to:

> protect fish and fishing places
> bring water to poor people
> stop the use of dangerous pesticides
> protect rainforests in Africa

They agreed that water, power, **health**, and growing food were all important things that the world needed to work on. Now different organizations have to work together to do these things.

Is it possible to make our planet greener? A lot of people will need to work hard to make it happen – countries, governments, families, even you and me. Every person in the world will need to help.

## A new idea

You have 75 billion dollars to spend on the world's problems over four years. What do you do with it? Where do you begin? What is the best way to spend the money?

In 2004 a group of people met in Copenhagen in Denmark to talk about this. They came from all over the world, and many of them were **experts** who knew about money, health, and water. These talks were called the Copenhagen **Consensus**, and after a week the group showed their answers to the world.

In 2008 they did the same thing again. What was at the top of their list? The group said that 60 million dollars will

buy **Vitamin** A for 140 million children in the poorest countries of the world. This will help them to be stronger and healthier; without Vitamin A, some children become **blind**. The group plans to meet every four years for more talks. Then they will give their list to governments and other organizations, who can use it to make plans for a better world.

## The world today

- Every minute, 252 people are born in the world, and 108 people die.
- Over 3 billion people – close to half the **population** of the world – live on less than two dollars fifty a day.
- 1.4 billion people live on less than one dollar a day.
- 1.3 billion people cannot get clean water.
- 2 billion people cannot get electricity.
- 3 billion do not have toilets that they can use.
- The 497 richest people in the world have 3.5 trillion dollars – more than 7% of all the money in use.
- 12% of the world's population uses 85% of its water.
- The richest 50 million people in Europe and North America have as much money as 2.7 billion poor people.

That is how the world is today. How about the future? Is it going to get better, or worse – or is it going to stay the same? What do you think?

**population** the number of people who live in one place

## READING CHECK

**Correct the mistakes in these sentences.**

**a** The carbon dioxide that people are taking out of the atmosphere is making problems for the world.

**b** If everyone tries to make their carbon footprint bigger, it will be better for the environment.

**c** If you want to make your carbon footprint smaller, it is better to travel by plane than by bicycle.

**d** The people who meet for the talks called the Copenhagen Consensus are a group of American teachers.

**e** The most important thing on the Copenhagen Consensus list in 2008 was more books for poor children.

**f** 12% of the world's population uses 85% of its electricity.

## WORD WORK

**Find words from Chapter 8 to match the underlined words.**

**a** Carbon dioxide goes into the air around the Earth and makes global warming. ...atmosphere...

**b** When you want to spend money on something important, ask someone who knows a lot about the subject if it's a good idea.

...........................

**c** New cars are expensive, but cars that belonged to another person before are cheaper. ...........................

**d** Babies need food that is full of things to make them healthy to grow up to be strong. ...........................

**e** Nearly half the world's number of people has less than two dollars a day each to live on. ...........................

**f** Clean water, good food, and how well and strong people are are very important things for people everywhere. ...........................

**g** If you don't get enough Vitamin A in your food, perhaps you will become not seeing. ...........................

**h** It isn't easy to arrive at a time when everyone says the same thing at the end of talks. ...........................

## WHAT NEXT?

**Here are two organizations that work to make a better world. Which would you like to learn more about? Why are you interested in them? Tick the boxes.**

### a ☐ Treepeople

A fifteen-year-old boy began this organization in 1973 in Los Angeles. They plant young trees all over the city to make it cooler and greener and to help stop flooding. Now a million people help in their work.

### b ☐ Interface Flooring

When Ray Anderson began his company Interface, he wanted to make carpet, and he wanted to make money. But his factories damaged the environment. One day Ray decided to change this. Now Interface uses power from the sun and from the wind, and they even make carpet squares from plant waste. They talk to other companies and help them to become greener, too.

## Project A — *National Parks*

**1   Read this information about the Great Barrier Reef and then answer the questions.**

# THE GREAT BARRIER REEF

**The Great Barrier Reef** is one of the world's wonders. It lies off the north-eastern coast of Australia, and is 2,300 kilometres long. That's longer than the west coast of the United States. In fact, if you go up in a rocket, you can see the Great Barrier Reef clearly from space.

Australia made the Great Barrier Reef into a Marine Park (a national park of the sea) in 1975. With 348,700 square kilometres of reefs, islands, beaches, and sea, the park is bigger than Italy.

In the park there are more than 2,900 reefs, more than 1,000 islands, and thousands of beaches. People come from all over the world to see the beautiful fish and sea plants here. There are 1,500 species of fish living on the reef, and 215 species of birds. If you come here in winter, you can see the humpback whales, as they swim up from Antarctica to have their babies. And there are dolphins here all through the year.

But like many beautiful places, the reef is in danger. Big fishing boats that pass the reef can easily damage the bottom of the sea and kill the fish and plants that live there. Large numbers of visitors often mean more rubbish and more damage to the reef. And changes in the weather mean that the sea is getting warmer now. Scientists are worried that warmer seas will kill the very small animals that make the reef.

**a**   Where is the Great Barrier Reef?

**b**   How long is the Great Barrier Reef?

**c**   When did the Great Barrier Reef become a national park?

**d**   How big is the Great Barrier Reef Marine Park?

**e**   What can you see at the reef?

**f**   What things can damage the reef?

**2** Read about the Sagarmatha National Park. 'Sagarmatha' is the Nepalese name for Mount Everest. Use the notes to complete the text below.

Where?  *around Mt Everest, north-east of Kathmandu, Nepal*
When?  *became National Park 1976*
How high Mt Everest?  *8,848 metres high*
How big?  *1,148 square kilometres — forests, rivers, mountains*
When to visit?  *Oct—Nov or March—May; warm days, cold nights. Dec—Feb; cold with heavy snow sometimes. June—Sept; lot of rain*
What to see?  *high mountains; glaciers (Khumbu and Lhotse) 3-5 kilometres long; forests below 4,500 metres; in summer — pink and red rhododendron trees*
What damage?  *rubbish from visitors, ice melting*

Sagarmatha National Park is .................. Kathmandu, Nepal.

It .................. in 1976, and it has .................. of forests, .................. . 'Sagarmatha' is the Nepalese name for Mount Everest, the .................. mountain in the world at .................. .

The best time to visit is .................. or .................. . Then, the days .................. but the nights .................. . If you come .................. it is usually .................. in the daytime, and sometimes there is .................. . From .................. there is .................. .

There is a lot to see here. There are many high mountains, and glaciers — rivers of ice — like .................. which are .................. . Up to 4,500 metres there are green .................. , and in summer you can see .................. .

Large numbers of visitors often mean more .................. and more .................. to the mountain. And changes to the weather mean that the .................. .

**3** Now write about a national park that you know, or would like to visit.

# Project B  *Environmental disaster*

**1** Here is some information about the *Prestige* oil spill that happened near the coast of northern Spain. Match the correct picture with each piece of information.

a ☐ The ship broke in half, and the two parts went to the bottom of the ocean. The oil tanker Prestige finally sank on Tuesday 19 November 2002.

b ☐ After a few days oil from the tanker arrived at the coast of north-west Spain. Soon there was black oil all over the beaches.

c ☐ The government sent boats out to sea with special barriers. Workers put the barriers on to the sea to stop more oil from going onto the beaches.

d ☐ People were worried about the birds and animals in the sea and on the beaches. They helped to find the birds with oil on them and take them for cleaning.

e ☐ Workers went onto the beaches with special machines to take the oil away. Other workers put on special suits to protect them from the oil.

f ☐ Later the government paid for a special small submarine to go to the Prestige. The Nautile went down to the Prestige and stopped some of the oil from coming out of holes in the tanker's side.

**1**

barrier

**2**

**2** **Make notes about another environmental disaster. You can choose one from this book, or another disaster that you know something about.**

Name of Disaster

Place                                                    Date

What happened?                              What did people do?

What happened to the environment?    How did they clean up?

What did the government do?              How much did it cost?

What must we do to make sure that it does not happen again?

**3** **Use your notes to make a project about the environmental disaster you have chosen. Use the project on pages 58–59 to help you.**

## GRAMMAR CHECK

**Sequencing words: at first, then, next, later, in the end, at the same time**

We use sequencing words to show the order in which things happen. Sequencing words usually come at the beginning of a sentence. We use at first for things that happen first. We use then, next, or later for things that follow. We use at the same time for things that happen at the same time, and we use in the end for things that come last.

*At first DDT killed the mosquitoes. Then the wasps died, too. Next the caterpillars started eating the grass roofs. Later the roofs fell down. At the same time the cats began to die and the rats made people ill. In the end more people were dying from the rats than from the mosquitoes.*

**1 Put the sentences in the correct order. Then complete the sentences with the sequencing words in the box.**

| at first    at the same time    in the end    later    next    ~~then~~ |
| --- |

**a** ...3... ...Then... the *Rainbow Warrior* arrived in Auckland.

**b** ...... ............... a photographer called Fernando Pereira died on the ship.

**c** ...... ............... Frédérique Bonlieu got a job in the Greenpeace office in Auckland.

**d** ...... ............... a French diver put something on the side of the ship.

**e** ...... ............... she was working for the French government.

**f** ...... ............... there was a big explosion on the ship.

**2 Match the sentence halves correctly.**

**a** At first the French government

**b** Then the Prime Minster

**c** Next Alain Mafart and Dominique Prieur

**d** At the same time France

**1** said that the government told two divers to attack the ship.

**2** had to pay New Zealand seven million dollars.

**3** said that they knew nothing about the attack.

**4** had to go to prison.

## GRAMMAR CHECK

**How much/many + uncountable/countable nouns**

We use how much and how many to ask about amounts and numbers. We use how much with uncountable nouns.

*How much rain falls in the rainforests every year?*

We use many with plural countable nouns.

*How many animals live in the top of the trees?*

**3** Complete the questions with *how much/many*. Then match the questions with the correct answers.

**a** ..How many.. parts of the world have rainforests? .....3..

**b** ..................... rain do the wettest rainforests get? ......

**c** ..................... plant species are there in the forests of Ecuador? ......

**d** ..................... medicines have come from the rainforests? ......

**e** ..................... golden toads are there in the world today? ......

**f** ..................... wildlife lived on Amchitka in 1971? ......

**g** ..................... money does Greenpeace make? ......

**h** ..................... people sailed on the *Phyllis Cormack* in 1971? ......

**i** ..................... violence do Greenpeace want people to use? ......

**j** ..................... boats have there been called *Rainbow Warrior*? ......

**1** Twelve.

**2** Hundreds.

**3** Three.

**4** None – no dollars, and no pounds.

**5** A lot of rain all year round.

**6** Two.

**7** More than 15,000.

**8** A lot.

**9** None since 1989.

**10** None against people, and none against countries.

## GRAMMAR CHECK

### Articles: a/an, the, no article (–)

We use the indefinite article a/an when we talk about singular nouns, when it is not clear which of several things we may mean.

*A penguin can stay under water for a long time.*

We use a in front of a word that begins with a consonant and an in front of a word that begins with a vowel or vowel sound.

*A polar bear can be 2 metres tall.*          *It is an Emperor penguin.*

We use the definite article the when we talk about singular and plural nouns, when it is clear which of several things we mean.

*The smoke from that factory is very black today.*

We do not use an article (–) when we talk about things in general.

*Penguins are very interesting animals.*          *Smoke is very bad for you.*

**4** **Complete the sentences with *a, an, the,* or –.**

   **a** Some of the most popular animals are ……–…. penguins.

   **b** ……… penguins that live in the Antarctic are Adélie and Emperor penguins.

   **c** ……… blue whale can be as much as 26 metres long.

   **d** People killed penguins because they had ……… oil in their bodies.

   **e** ……… clownfish in the film *Finding Nemo* was called Nemo.

   **f** The warm waters near Australia and the Philippines have ……… clownfish.

   **g** A popular fish for children in the United States is ……… clownfish.

   **h** Water that is hard because it is very cold is ……… ice.

   **i** ……… ice in the Arctic is melting earlier now.

   **j** ……… polar bear can live with little food in the summer months.

   **k** ……… polar bears wait on the ice to catch seals.

   **l** ……… seal is a good meal for a polar bear.

   **m** ……… Emperor penguin can stay at sea for a month.

## GRAMMAR CHECK

**Linkers: and, but, because, or, so**

Linkers are words that join two sentences together to make one. We use and to link two parts of a sentence with the same idea.

*The rocket left the ground and took Envisat up into the sky.*

We use but to link two parts of a sentence with different ideas.

*Darwin travelled on the* Beagle, *but he didn't get any money for his work.*

We use because to show the reason for something.

*Envisat can send information to the Earth because it gets power from the sun.*

We use or to give a different possibility.

*Envisat can see the beginnings of storms, or it can see fires in the forests.*

We use so to show the result of something.

*The scientists got the rocket working again, so it left the Earth on 1 March.*

**5  Complete the sentences. Use the words in the box.**

| so   or   and   because   and   ~~but~~   or   so   because   but |
|---|

**a**  Envisat was ready, .....*but*.... there was something wrong with the rocket.

**b**  Finches can have big strong bills, ............... they can have narrow bills.

**c**  The *Beagle* went to South America, ............... it went to the Galapagos Island.

**d**  Darwin was interested in plants and animals, ............... he agreed to travel on the *Beagle*.

**e**  The finches' beaks were different ............... they ate different food.

**f**  1,250 copies of *The Origin of Species* arrived in the bookshops, ............... they all sold on the first day.

**g**  Some people got very angry about the book ............... they did not agree with it.

**h**  Things in the environment can change quickly, ............... they can change slowly.

**i**  Some animals learned to change with the environment, ............... others did not.

**j**  People are getting more interested in the environment, ............... they are asking more questions about it.

## GRAMMAR CHECK

**Gerund as subject or object**

We can use the gerund as the subject or object of a verb. To make the gerund, we usually add –ing to the verb, but when a verb ends in a consonant + –e, we remove the –e and add –ing.

*Walking is better for the environment than driving.* (= subject)

*I'm going to stop driving.* (= object)

**The gerund can have its own object.**

*Riding a bicycle is good for the environment.*

*People need to stop polluting the Earth.*

**6 Complete the sentences with the gerund (–*ing*) form of the verbs in the box.**

| | | | | | | |
|---|---|---|---|---|---|---|
| drink | drive | eat | pay | walk | give | help |
| grow | look | ~~put~~ | think | travel | turn | hunt |

**a** ..Putting. carbon dioxide into the atmosphere makes global warming worse.

**b** Some people have begun ............... by plane less than before.

**c** ............... a lot of meat means that you have a bigger carbon footprint.

**d** ............... a small car, not a large car, helps the environment.

**e** If you can, stop ............... bottled water.

**f** A lot of people enjoy ...............
vegetables for themselves.

**g** ............... for clothes in second-hand
shops is a good idea.

**h** ............... Vitamin A to poor children
helps them not to go blind.

**i** ............... off the light when you leave a
room saves electricity.

**j** Everyone needs to start ...............
before they buy things.

**k** The Earth Summits were all about ............... the environment.

**l** ............... to school or work is good for the you and for the environment.

**m** ............... animals is not possible in National Parks.

**n** Greenpeace thinks that ............... poor countries to take nuclear waste is dangerous.

## GRAMMAR CHECK

**Forming questions: Present and Past Simple, Present and Past Continuous**

To form questions using the Present Simple and the Past Simple, we use do/does + subject + infinitive without to.

*Envisat gets power from the sun.*     *How does Envisat get power?*

*Emperor penguins live in the Antarctic. Where do Emperor penguins live?*

To form questions using the Past Simple, we use did + subject + infinitive without to.

*Darwin looked at small birds called finches. What did Darwin look at?*

To form questions using the Present Continuous, we use am/is/are + subject + the –ing form of the verb.

*The environment is changing all the time. What is the environment doing?*

To form questions using the Past Continuous, we use was/were + subject + the –ing form of the verb.

*At the age of nine, Chico Mendes was tapping rubber. When was Chico Mendes tapping rubber?*

**7 Complete the questions. Use the subjects, and the Present or Past Simple, or Present and Past Continuous forms of the verbs in brackets.**

**a** What do Nadezdha and her family find (Nadezdha and her family/find) hard to forget? The Chernobyl disaster.

**b** Where ............................................................. (Nadezdha/live) now? She lives in Igovka.

**c** Where ............................................. (she/live) in 1986? She was living in Borshchyovka.

**d** How ............................................. (she/hear) about the disaster? She heard about it on the radio.

**e** When ............................................. (the last villagers/leave) Borshchyovka? They left on 4 May.

**f** What ............................................. (Nadezdha/find) in her house when she went back? She didn't find anything that was there before.

**g** What ............................................. (she/do) now when she remembers the past? She shakes.

**h** How ............................................. (people/make) electricity now in some countries? They are making it from the wind or the power of the sea.

## GRAMMAR CHECK

**If clauses**

We can use if clauses to talk about a condition – something that must happen so that another thing can happen. In this case, we use the present tense in the *if* clause and can/can't in the main clause.

*If we start working now, we can slow down global warming.*

We can also use *if* clauses to talk about a future possibility. In this case, we use the present tense in the *if* clause, and will/won't in the main clause.

*If we plant a lot of trees, the city will be cooler and greener.*

**8 Complete the sentences. Use the correct form of the verbs in brackets.**

**a** If polar bears ..don't eat.. (not eat) lots of seals in the winter, they can't live through the summer.

**b** If scientists breed clownfish, people ..................... (not catch) the wild fish to sell them.

**c** If a big storm or flood ..................... (begin) to happen, Envisat can send information about it back to the Earth.

**d** If you ..................... (put) a lot of pesticides into the Earth and water, some of them ..................... (go) into your food.

**e** If there ..................... (be) only a small number of animals of one species, that species can easily disappear.

**f** If the Pantera organization ..................... (learn) about big cats in danger, it will work to save them.

**g** If people in Chenega Bay get food from the sea, they ..................... (not be) sure that it is safe.

**h** If an Emperor penguin dives under the water, it ..................... (stay) there for eleven minutes.

**i** If fishermen ..................... (catch) dolphins in their net, the animals can die.

# DOMINOES  THE STRUCTURED APPROACH TO READING IN ENGLISH

*Dominoes* is an enjoyable series of illustrated classic and modern stories in four carefully graded language stages – from Starter to Three – which take learners from beginner to intermediate level.

Each *Domino* reader includes:

- **a good story** to read and enjoy
- **integrated activities** to develop reading skills and increase active vocabulary
- **personalized projects** to make the language and story themes more meaningful
- **seven pages of grammar activities** for consolidation.

Each *Domino* pack contains a reader, plus a MultiROM with:

- **a complete audio recording of the story**, fully dramatized to bring it to life
- **interactive activities** to offer further practice in reading and language skills and to consolidate learning.

If you liked this Level Two *Domino*, why not read these?

### White Fang

*Jack London*

Life is hard and dangerous for both people and animals in the frozen Canadian North. For a wolf like White Fang it is a continuous fight to find food – a fight in which many animals die.

When White Fang meets the people of the North – first Indians and then White Men – he learns to live with them like a dog. But some men are cruel to their dogs and others are kind. Will White Fang's life be any easier now?

**Book ISBN: 978 0 19 424882 2**
**MultiROM Pack ISBN: 978 0 19 424834 1**

### Emma

*Jane Austen*

Emma Woodhouse is beautiful, clever, and rich. She lives alone with her father, and spends a lot of her time thinking about future husbands – for her friends. When she meets Harriet Smith, a poor girl with no family, Emma decides that she must find a husband for her. Harriet is pleased to be Emma's friend – but will Emma's matchmaking make Harriet happy?

**Book ISBN: 978 0 19 424884 6**
**MultiROM Pack ISBN: 978 0 19 424836 5**

You can find details and a full list of books in the *Dominoes* catalogue and Oxford English Language Teaching Catalogue, and on the website: www.oup.com/elt

Teachers: see www.oup.com/elt for a full range of online support, or consult your local office.

| | CEFR | Cambridge Exams | IELTS | TOEFL iBT | TOEIC |
|---|---|---|---|---|---|
| Level 3 | B1 | PET | 4.0 | 57-86 | 550 |
| Level 2 | A2–B1 | KET-PET | 3.0-4.0 | – | – |
| Level 1 | A1–A2 | YLE Flyers/KET | 3.0 | – | – |
| Starter & Quick Starter | A1 | YLE Movers | – | – | – |